Adhd in boys :
What to know about ADHD in boys

Lucas Olle

Table of content

Chapter 1

What to know about adhd in boys

Attention deficit hyperactivity disorder (ADHD) is a prevalent neuropsychiatric illness. Boys tend to obtain more ADHD diagnoses than girls. This is likely owing to the way the symptoms of ADHD manifest in each group.

Around 8.4% of children and 2.5% of adults have ADHD, according to the American Psychiatric Association.

Doctors diagnose ADHD more typically in males than girls. In fact, about three times as many males obtain an ADHD diagnosis as girls. School-age children commonly obtain a diagnosis when they become disruptive in the classroom.

ADHD impacts the way a person thinks, feels, and behaves. The illness might make it difficult to concentrate on projects for lengthy periods of time or keep track of items such as school assignments.

Boys with an ADHD diagnosis may be more restless, impulsive, and hyperactive than their classmates. They may also have problems focusing, find it hard to stay sitting in school, or experience learning deficits.

Keep reading to discover more about ADHD in males and how it varies from the illness in girls. This article will also look at the therapy options available and how parents and carers may assist manage the disease.

At a glance\sBoys are more likely to be hyperactive than females.

They're also more likely than females to be diagnosed with ADHD.

Boys with ADHD might confront specific social obstacles.

"ADHD is basically about being hyper." "It's something only guys have."

What are some signs of ADHD?

These are two of the numerous misconceptions regarding ADHD. There's a germ of truth behind them, though: Even though boys and girls are equally as likely to have ADHD, males are more likely than girls to be diagnosed with ADHD.

The explanation is that guys commonly experience hyperactivity as a symptom – more so than girls. And hyperactivity might be easier to recognize than other ADHD symptoms.

What ADHD looks like in males

Boys and girls may display many of the same indicators of ADHD. But males are more likely to be hyperactive, and their conduct is impossible to ignore. Here's what you could see:

Running and screaming while playing, even inside

Playing too harshly

Bumping into people and objects

Constantly moving even while sat

This sort of conduct is more likely to raise flags at home and in the school than other ADHD indicators, such difficulties with attention. So guys are more likely than girls to be diagnosed with ADHD in childhood.

Not all guys with ADHD are hyperactive, either. Some may merely have impulsivity and inattention, the other main symptoms of ADHD.

Boys with ADHD frequently get called out or chastised for their hyperactive and impulsive conduct. They may get into problems a lot at home and at school. And their conduct might turn off other youngsters and make it challenging to blend in socially.

Every kid with ADHD is unique. There are plenty of guys with ADHD who suffer with other ADHD difficulties, such difficulty concentrating. But in many circumstances, the experience of ADHD for males may be extremely different from the experience for girls.

ADHD behavior and "being bad"

Kids with ADHD who are energetic and impulsive frequently get attention. This might be beneficial and terrible. Good because their ADHD is more likely to be recognized and treated early on. Bad because their conduct frequently lands them in trouble.

They could receive a lot of negative criticism from instructors, siblings, coaches, and other families. That can be incredibly distressing. It may take a toll on kids' self-esteem and make them act out more, which can lead to disciplinary difficulties.

Hyperactivity may be a significant concern for guys. But bear in mind that some males with ADHD aren't hyperactive. There may be a consequence to it, too.

Because they don't match the norm, guys who aren't hyperactive are more likely to go missed (just as girls are) (much like girls are). They may not receive the unwanted attention, but they also may not get the help they need.

Chapter 2

ADHD and problems establishing friends

Many youngsters with ADHD have problems making friends and fitting in. Boys confront a particular set of societal obstacles, though.

They're typically supposed to be tough and roll with the punches. But many youngsters with ADHD have problems controlling their emotions. And they don't always understand a social setting the proper way.

Sometimes, guys with ADHD act like the class clown to conceal their struggles and be popular with other youngsters. That conduct may backfire, though. Their antics might be hilarious, but youngsters could also find them bothersome.

Talking frankly about social issues may help kids comprehend what's occurring — and help you determine how best to assist.

The Top 10 Manifestations of ADHD in Boys The characteristic signs of ADHD in guys are not hyperactivity and impulsivity. Especially in the teenage years, they are poor perspective taking, rejection sensitive dysphoria, inadequate episodic memory, and these other 7 ADHD features.

1. Difficulty with Self-Directed Speak\s"We all have an internal dialog in our thoughts that we utilize to talk to ourselves. When someone has ADHD, they are not always hearing that internal conversation or 'brain coach.' When your brain functions with ADHD, the volume on your brain coach is turned down too low. The self-directed

conversation is there; they simply aren't hearing it very well."

2. Hyperfocusing on Things That Are Interesting and Difficulty Sustaining Attention on Things That Are Not

"Parents say to me, 'How can I assist my kid focus better?' I have never found anything that helps for this other than medicine and helping kids build their self-directed dialog, and that's a lengthy process. If your kid tends to hyperfocus on things that are intriguing to him, it might help him become extremely successful in life."

3. Weak Episodic Memory\s"Kids with ADHD have trouble recalling prior events and the emotions linked with those past experiences. If you've explained something to your kid, and he claims he doesn't remember how to do it, that may be true."

4. Poor Future Thinking Skills\s"People with ADHD have difficulties imagining things in the future since they prefer to live in the present. If you've ever said to your kid, 'If you finish your homework every

night this week, you can have a reward on Friday night,' and it didn't work, it was because the incentive was too far in the future."

5. Difficulties Sensing the Passage of Time\s"People with ADHD have difficulty perceiving time as a real idea. Often, they would spend more time debating over a job than it would really take to perform the work since they have problems understanding how much time is required."

6. Inconsistent Situational Awareness\s"I can situational awareness 'reading the field' with youngsters. This is how we take multiple bits of information from our surroundings, put them together as a whole, and construct meaning from them. If someone has difficulties recognizing the wider picture because they concentrate on the minute details, they will likely have problems with situational awareness."

7. Poor Perspective Taking Skills\s"If your kid has problems reading social signals, it suggests he actually has trouble with

perspective taking – understanding other's thoughts and emotions, and recognizing how he comes across to others. It's not that your youngster lacks empathy; it's that he lacks perspective taking skills."

8. Trouble Putting Problem Scale in a Relevant Context\s"This is why youngsters with ADHD may over-react or under-react to the size of the problem."

9. Difficulty with Unexpected Change

"When kids have to do things like get off video games to start schoolwork, it is incredibly tough because they are moving from a liked job to a non-preferred one without time to prepare for that."

10. Rejection Sensitive Dysphoria

"People with ADHD have a predisposition to react emotionally to perceived or real rejection. People with ADHD tend to live in high emotions and have a strong response to receiving rejection. The reverse of this is Recognition Response Euphoria. People with ADHD tend to be highly sensitive to praise and recognition when it is intentional and helps a youngster identify their qualities in themselves — not when it is empty. Give your kid recognition for things that demand effort."

Chapter 3

How Is ADHD Diagnosed in Boys?

While guys tend to have more disruptive symptoms of ADHD, not every male kid will present this way. Where a young person is suspected of living with ADHD, healthcare practitioners may apply recommendations established by the American Psychiatric Association's Diagnostic and Statistical Manual (DSM-5) (DSM-5).

To be diagnosed with this illness, you will observe a continuous pattern of inattention, hyperactivity, or impulsiveness.

Inattention

Inattentive symptoms may include:

Poor attention to detail or making readily preventable errors throughout activities1

Difficulty with lengthy periods of concentration

Difficulty organizing tasks and activities

Disliking tasks that involve mental exertion such as school assignments

Getting sidetracked easily

Forgetfulness

Hyperactivity and Impulsivity

Hyperactive and impulsive symptoms may include:1

Excessive fidgeting

Difficulty keeping sitting

Excessive talking

Interrupting people whilst speaking

Running about in inappropriate places

Highly energetic

Blurting out the answer to an unfinished question

Six or more symptoms need to be present in minors 16 and younger, and five or more for those seventeen and older. The symptoms need to be present for six months, create difficulty in functioning in two or more places such as home, school, or job, and have been present before the age of 12.

Clinicians may typically employ psychological tests and questionnaires in addition to the history and examination to achieve an appropriate ADHD diagnosis.

How is ADHD in males different from girls?

Doctors diagnose and treat ADHD more commonly in males than in girls because the symptoms in boys might be more obvious and disturbing for others.

Externalizing behaviors connected to ADHD are often more frequent in school-age males than internalizing behaviors, which are more commonly found in girls. Practitioners are, consequently, more prone to classify classroom hyperactive behaviors as ADHD in guys.

This is a form of inherent bias in diagnosis. In reality, the ratio of males with an ADHD diagnosis compared with the number of girls is 3:1\s, and it may be as high as 9:1 in certain regions.

Girls with ADHD often have less hyperactive and impulsive symptoms and more inattentive symptoms. Because of this, females with ADHD, although inattentive, are less disruptive. This is particularly noticeable during school hours, since ADHD is easier to recognize.

Teachers, therefore, prefer to suggest guys for ADHD treatment more frequently than girls because of the more serious disruption that boys' actions may create.

Some study also shows that because ADHD is not as outwardly visible in females, they frequently go without an ADHD diagnosis while having the illness. Adults and school-age peers may sometimes see females with hyperactive-impulsive characteristics as overemotional, demanding, or too chatty. Girls may often strive hard to disguise their symptoms.

Chapter 4

Signs and symptoms

ADHD is one of the most common\s pediatric neuropsychiatric illnesses. Its characteristic qualities are hyperactivity, inattention, and impulsivity.

Those with ADHD likely to exhibit a mix of these symptoms\s:

making errors in activities such as homework\sdisliking or avoiding things that demand continual mental effort

not listening when talked to directly\sforgetting regular chores not following through on instructions\sdifficulty keeping attention\slosing items regularly\sbeing easily distracted\sdifficulty arranging chores and activities

Some indications of hyperactivity and impulsivity include:\sfidgeting while seated\shaving trouble waiting for one's turn\sinterrupting others when they talk\snot being able to play quietly\sfinding it difficult to remain seated\srunning or climbing in unsuitable settings

being continuously in motion\stalking endlessly

However, these activities are not entirely indications of ADHD. This makes delivering an accurate diagnosis more complex.

Impaired self-regulation is frequent among persons with ADHD. Self-regulation entails a person regulating and controlling their emotions and actions in an acceptable manner for a specific setting.

Some characteristics of self-regulation include calming oneself down when disturbed, controlling impatience without an outburst, rejecting highly emotional responses to disturbing stimuli, and responding to changes in expectations.

ADHD is usually considered as a disorder that affects guys. In actuality, there's a possibility each sex is equally impacted by the illness. However, because of the behavioral characteristics that may be more pronounced in males, it is typically called a male-dominated illness. 3

Some study has identified a slight difference between teenage males and girls in how they manage their ADHD, with girls showing lower self-efficacy and worse coping skills than boys. However, by age, these disparities tend to balance out. 3

While females with this illness may struggle with self-esteem, this behavior is less frequent in guys. Likewise, females may discover that they are profoundly impacted by distinct adverse life situations, but guys may feel less passionately about identical occurrences. 3

Some research reveal that males tend to display more externalizing symptoms such as violence, while girls may express greater rates of despair and anxiety. Such guys with ADHD are more likely to be branded as rule-breakers at school, home, or other social situations.

Chapter 5

Benefits of ADHD in boys

Although ADHD comes with several obstacles, there are also some possible perks and abilities that might result from having the illness.

For example, guys with ADHD may be more creative, particularly while completing a goal-driven task.

In one 2017 study, for instance, researchers recruited 71 adult participants with ADHD and 36 control individuals. They observed that both groups created a comparable amount of ideas when given a task, with no difference in originality, regardless matter their ADHD diagnosis.

However, when the researchers alerted the participants to a possible bonus, the persons with ADHD generated more suggestions than those in the control group.

The researchers were not quite convinced of the processes involved. Still, the results revealed that persons with ADHD may do better than their counterparts when they strive toward a goal — especially if they pursue an area that suits their talents and passion.

Although this research featured adults, it is plausible to assume comparable results among younger boys and girls. That stated, the adult individuals may have had to build these abilities during later cognitive growth periods to compensate for the problems of learning throughout infancy.

Some additional possible advantages of having ADHD include:

spontaneity\scourage\shigh energy\sconversational skills

How Does ADHD Affect Boys?

ADHD tends to show with a more aggressive, energetic aspect in guys. They may struggle with their classmates at school and might demonstrate stubborn or rule-breaking conduct.

ADHD may lead to a more injury-prone existence in males. Teenagers with this illness are more prone to smoke, drink, or experiment with drugs. It isn't unusual for them to come into some troubles with the law.

Children with ADHD might potentially develop other mental illnesses such as depression and anxiety disorders.

Boys 2 Men: When ADHD and Puberty Collide

What parents of males with ADHD should look for as their kids navigate through puberty.

Until he was 10 or 11, Robert was joyful and vivacious, albeit occasionally distractible and hyper.

Then came 12 and 13. "He bounces between couch potato and monster," adds his mother, Anne. "What happened to my darling little boy?"

What transpired were puberty (physical changes) and adolescence (psychological and social changes), which occur when children begin evolving into adults. Some youngsters begin to "act" like adolescents before puberty; others may not embrace the position of adolescent until well beyond puberty. Whenever they happen, you're in for a rocky journey.

Fortunately, guys with attention deficit disorder (ADHD or ADD) don't appear to have greater trouble dealing with puberty than other teenagers with ADHD. However, their individual issues and strains may vary substantially. Here are some topics to consider.

Refusing Medicine

"Raging hormones" may produce profound physical and psychological changes. Teens typically find physical changes disturbing and want want to fit in. That's why many youngsters who willingly took medicine in elementary school began to complain and rebel in their teens; they don't want to be marked out by going to the school office or health room.

Try to understand and assist. If you can discover an acceptable drug in a long-acting formulation, your kid won't have to take medicine in school. You may even allow a brief trial off medicine which may assist your youngster comprehend the necessity to continue taking it. Before quitting medication, contact with your family doctor or a mental health specialist.

Peer Pressure

All youngsters need to feel accepted by their peer group. If the years of having ADHD (and maybe a cognitive handicap) have resulted in poor social skills and limited success with peers, early adolescence may be difficult.

The concern for some youngsters is that they may seek out any peer group that welcomes them. Socially rejected guys with ADHD usually latch on to other "misfits" who do not perform well in school or athletics. The combination of a misfit social group, the urge to be liked, and poor self-esteem placed kids with ADHD at significant risk of alcohol and drug use. Get educated and if you suspect these problems, get help.

Lack of Supervision

Experimentation with booze, drugs, and sex doesn't take place on weekend evenings. The riskiest hours are between 3 and 6 P.M. on school days. Kids are typically unattended because both parents work. They routinely visit friends' residences with no adult present.

Be proactive. If you can't watch your adolescents after school, make sure they're participating in sports, arts, community service or other activities that are supervised by adults. Keep tabs on where they are and what they're doing at all times.

Comorbid Disorders

People with ADHD are at higher risk of comorbid disorders (two or more symptoms that occur at the same time) (two or more conditions that occur at the same time). Mood and anxiety problems frequently initially show up between the ages of 8 and 12, then again in early adolescence. Watch your kid for signs, and get assistance if you suspect there's a problem.

Also check for indicators of Conduct Disorder and Oppositional Defiant Disorder, which are characterised by antisocial, confrontational, and abnormally oppositional conduct.

These illnesses typically position impulsive boys in risky, even criminal circumstances. Intervention is necessary.

Medication Changes

Most boys on ADHD medication do not need to alter medication when they hit puberty. Even considerable weight gains may not require an additional dosage. If the dosage used earlier in life still works, don't modify it.

The good news is that around half of youngsters with ADHD recover dramatically after puberty. Many no longer require medicine. The remainder will definitely require medication through puberty and maybe into maturity.

On balance, most guys with ADHD navigate through puberty with little more difficulty than others. Becoming a couch potato is not a disorder. However, seek expert assistance if your kid looks abnormally depressed, distant, aggressive, or nervous. Don't wait for an issue to evolve into a catastrophe. Even if your fears are unjustified, it's better to share them with a mental health expert than to wish you had acted sooner.

www.ingramcontent.com/pod-product-compliance
Lightning Source LLC
Chambersburg PA
CBHW071459150726
48000CB00006B/2628